America the Beautiful

The Story Behind Our National Hymm

CHELSEA CLUBHOUSE

An Imprint of Chelsea House Publishers

A Haights Cross Communications Company

Philadelphia

Liz Sonneborn

Chelsea Clubhouse books are published by
Chelsea House Publishers, a subsidiary of
Haights Cross Communications Company

A Haights Cross Communications ◆ Company

The Chelsea House World Wide Web address is
www.chelseahouse.com

Printed and bound in the United States of America.

9 8 7 6 5 4 3 2 1

Library of Congress Cataloging-in-Publication Data
Sonneborn, Liz.
  America the beautiful : the story behind our national hymn / by
Liz Sonneborn.
      p. cm. — (America in words and song)
Summary: Introduces Katharine Bates and Samuel Ward, who wrote
America the Beautiful, and explores the meaning of the words, how
they relate to American history, and why the song became a
favorite patriotic anthem.
Includes bibliographical references and index.
  ISBN 0-7910-7332-7
  1. Bates, Katharine Lee, 1859-1929. America the beautiful—
Juvenile literature. 2. Ward, Samuel A., 1847-1903. America the
beautiful—Juvenile literature. 3. National songs—United States—
History and criticism—Juvenile literature. [1. Bates, Katharine Lee,
1859-1929. America the beautiful. 2. Ward, Samuel A., 1847-1903.
3. National songs—United States—History and criticism.] I. Title.
II. Series.
  PS1077.B4A839 2004
  811'.4—dc21
                                                    2003004033

Selected Sources

Bates, Katharine Lee. *America the Beautiful and Other Poems.*
    New York: Thomas Y. Crowell, 1911.

History Resource Center. Farmington Hills, MI: Gale Group.
    http://galenet.galegroup.com/servlet/HistRC/

Molotsky, Irvin. *The Flag, the Poet and the Song: The Story of
    the Star-Spangled Banner.* New York: Dutton, 2001.

Sherr, Lynn. *America the Beautiful: The Stirring True Story
    Behind Our Nation's Favorite Song.* New York: Public Affairs,
    2001.

Editorial Credits

Colleen Sexton, editor; Takeshi Takahashi, designer;
Mary Englar, photo researcher

Content Reviewer

Carolyn Powers, Executive Director, Falmouth Historical
Society, Falmouth, Massachusetts

Photo Credits

Table of Contents

Introduction

Nearly a century has passed since Americans first heard "America the Beautiful." From the beginning, people embraced its uplifting music and spirited words. It quickly became a beloved **patriotic** song. Some people say the song has such great meaning that it gives them chills or brings tears to their eyes.

"America the Beautiful" is a joyful song that celebrates a great nation. It honors government officials when they are sworn into office. People sing it at graduation ceremonies, religious services, and sporting events. The song has long been a favorite of many famous performers, including singers Ray Charles and Tony Bennett.

Students sing "America the Beautiful" at a memorial service honoring those who were killed in the September 11, 2001, terrorist attacks.

In times of national crisis, "America the Beautiful" offers comfort and hope. During World War I (1914–1918), soldiers carried pocket-sized songbooks that included the song. Seeking strength, Americans sang it after Japanese forces bombed Pearl Harbor, Hawaii, during World War II (1939–1945), and after President John F. Kennedy was killed in 1963. When terrorist attacks in America killed nearly 3,000 people on September 11, 2001, "America the Beautiful" calmed the fears of the nation.

The story of "America the Beautiful" began more than 100 years ago. The song came into being almost by accident. In fact, the two people responsible for the song—a poet and a composer—never met. Nevertheless, they created one of America's best-loved patriotic tunes, a song now considered our national **hymn.**

"Who can sing now, with the same meaning we had before, one stanza of ["America the Beautiful"] that goes, '[O] beautiful for patriot's dream, that sees beyond the years, thine alabaster cities gleam, undimmed by human tears.' We can never sing that song again, that way…"
—CBS news anchor Dan Rather, reacting to the terrorist attacks of September 11, 2001

5

The Poet

Known for teaching spirited English classes at Wellesley College, Katharine Lee Bates was also a poet with a great imagination.

On a June afternoon in 1893, a young **professor** boarded a train in Boston, Massachusetts. Her name was Katharine Lee Bates. A native of Falmouth, Massachusetts, Bates taught English at Wellesley College, an all-women's school just southwest of Boston. Among her students, Bates was well known for her clever wit and endless curiosity.

Months before, the 33-year-old Bates had been invited to spend three weeks teaching summer school at Colorado College. She jumped at the chance. Bates was excited by any opportunity to travel. As always, she brought along her journal to jot down her thoughts.

After her first night on the train, Bates woke up in Niagara Falls. People from all over the world came to western New York to see these beautiful waterfalls. Greatly moved by the thundering waters that cast up great clouds of mist, Bates wrote about "the glory and music of Niagara Falls."

Her next stop was Chicago, Illinois. There, she stayed at the family home of another Wellesley professor, Katharine Coman. Miss Coman, too, was going to spend the summer teaching at Colorado College. Before continuing west, the two friends visited the World's Columbian **Exposition.** This great "World's Fair" included more than 65,000 exhibits and was attended by more than 27 million people. To Bates, the most striking exhibit was the White City. This complex of white buildings, which gleamed in the sun, was meant to represent the future of architecture.

Katharine Lee Bates made her first stop at Niagara Falls, which she called "a splendid thrill of glory and of peril."

At the World's Columbian Exposition, the shining buildings of the White City captivated Bates. She wrote that the fair was "a thing of beauty."

On July 3, the two Katharines headed off to Colorado by train. From the window, Bates saw many beautiful sights. The endless fields of Kansas particularly struck her. Golden wheat, lit by the sun, trembled in the summer wind. Bates wrote that the view gave her a "quickened and deepened sense of America."

On July 5, the two women arrived in Colorado Springs, the home of Colorado College. Bates was drawn to the area's natural beauty right away. The town sat on the eastern edge of the Rockies, the longest mountain range in North America. In her free time, Bates visited the area's canyons, bluffs, and giant rock formations.

Bates wrote that July 22 was the "supreme day of our Colorado **sojourn.**" On that day, she and several friends traveled up a mountain on mule-pulled carts. Called Pikes Peak, the mountain stretched high into the clouds.

As her train chugged across Kansas, Bates admired vast fields of golden wheat.

Mule carts (below) carried sightseers up Pikes Peak (above). Katharine Lee Bates called the view from the top the "most glorious scenery I ever beheld."

As the air thinned at the mountaintop, several of her friends became sick and fainted. Bates, however, was more overwhelmed by the view. To the west, the peaks of the Rockies appeared purple in the sun. To the east, lay a broad plain. Bates was thrilled "looking out over the sea-like expanse of fertile country spreading away so far under those ample skies." At that moment, her head filled with the opening lines of "America the Beautiful"—the poem that would make her famous.

The Composer

Samuel Ward discovered his talent for music at an early age. He learned to play the accordian when he was 6 years old and became a skillful organist by the time he was a teenager.

One hot summer day, 33-year-old Samuel Augustus Ward went on an outing. With a friend, Harry Martin, he left his home in Newark, New Jersey, and boarded a steamboat. The boat took the friends to Coney Island in Brooklyn, New York. The year was 1882, 11 years before Katharine Lee Bates made her trip up Pikes Peak.

At that time, there was no air conditioning. When the temperature rose, the best way to escape the heat was to go to the beach. The beach resort at Coney Island was especially popular with people in New York City and Newark. After a short trip by boat or train, visitors could spend the day enjoying the cool ocean breeze.

Coney Island had many other attractions. People could stroll along the seaside boardwalk. Or they could stop and listen to live bands playing the popular songs of the day. Some visitors swam in the ocean, while others feasted on hot dogs and other Coney Island treats.

In the late 1800s, cool beaches, delicious food, and a variety of entertainment drew crowds of city-dwellers to Coney Island.

Steamboats carried many visitors to and from Coney Island. It was on a return journey that Samuel Ward's head filled with the melody for what would become "America the Beautiful."

It's not known exactly what Ward and Martin did during their day at the beach. But Ward later shared with relatives what happened on their way home. On the steamboat heading for Newark, the two men listened to a two-piece orchestra playing on the deck. Sam Ward began to hum. Suddenly, he asked Martin for a piece of paper. A tune had popped into Ward's head, and he wanted to write it down. Martin checked his pockets, but they were empty. Finally, he removed the detachable cuff from his shirt and handed it to his friend. Ward quickly scribbled musical notes on the cuff, capturing the music playing in his head.

Sam Ward was a well-known businessman in Newark. He owned three successful stores that sold pianos, organs, and sheet music. But Ward's first love was making music. In addition to composing songs, he was the organist at Newark's Grace Church. He also founded the Orpheus Society, a men's singing group whose performances continue to thrill audiences today.

At the organ in Grace Church, Ward played the tune he wrote on Harry Martin's cuff. The composer called it "Materna." He paired it with the words from "O Mother Dear, Jerusalem," an old verse based on Biblical texts. A chorus of 200 men and boys gave the first public performance of the song.

"Materna" became a favorite hymn of churchgoers. In July 1888, the song was published in *The Parish Choir*, a magazine that featured church music. Soon after, the song appeared in **hymnals** published throughout the country. Ward was a humble man, but even he admired his work. He

First published in 1888, Ward's "Materna" was paired with the words of the old verse "O Mother Dear, Jerusalem." Ward composed other hymns during his lifetime, but none were as popular as this one.

once wrote of hearing a children's choir singing the song and marveling at "how beautiful my melody is."

The Song

Sam Ward believed that composing "Materna" was one of his greatest achievements. In his hometown of Newark, the song earned him a measure of fame. When he died in 1903, his **obituary** called him "one of the best known musical men in the State." Ward, however, didn't live to see his work become one of the best-loved songs in all of America.

While Ward's "Materna" was already a well-known hymn, Bates's poem was just gaining attention. The great rise in its popularity began November 19, 1904. On that day, "America the Beautiful" was printed in the *Boston Evening Transcript*. It was the most widely read newspaper in New England.

Katharine Lee Bates's poem became popular after this article appeared in the *Boston Evening Transcript* in 1904.

We rather guess that Professor Katherine Lee Bates of Wellesley has written the American national hymn; that is to say, if now it can be wedded to music of its own quality. Smith's "America" is fixed beyond recovery in an English tune, and the British national hymn at that. Keller's American hymn has now one set of verses and now another, the best of all being, of course, Dr. O. W. Holmes's "Angel of Peace," written for the Peace Jubilee. Julius Eichberg's "American Hymn" was given words smacking of a German adaptation. Now here is a thoroughly American production well-nigh perfect as poetry, and in the most exalted strain as politics. America has only to live up to the aspirations here breathed to realize its Golden Age,—the Golden Age of those idealists of late held in scant respect, the Fathers of the Declaration and the Constitution. As for what may be considered the physiography of the poem, Smith's Miltonic picture in those supposedly matchless lines

"I love thy rocks and rills
Thy woods and templed hills"

is fairly mated by Miss Bates's:

"O beautiful for spacious skies,
For amber waves of grain,
For purple mountain majesties
Above the fruitful plain!"

Then the course of national history is "touched in," as artists say, with not less of comprehensive and literal truth than of fine poetic imagery, in the next verse:

O beautiful for pilgrim feet,
Whose stern, impassioned stress
A thoroughfare for freedom beat
Across the wilderness!
America! America!
God mend thine every flaw,
Confirm thy soul in self-control,
Thy liberty in law!

And now comes the most beautiful and exalted of all the hymn's nobility of thought, uttering the patriot's prayer and faith in America's perfectibility:

O beautiful for glory-tale
Of liberating strife,
When valiantly, for man's avail,
Men lavished precious life!
America! America!
May God thy gold refine
Till all success be nobleness,
And every gain divine!

O beautiful for patriot dream
That sees beyond the years
Thine alabaster cities gleam
Undimmed by human tears!
America! America!
God shed his grace on thee,
And crown thy good with brotherhood
From sea to shining sea!

Have we an American composer to fit this noble poem to music "not too good for human nature's daily food," and so make the whole the "one entire and perfect chrysolite" of a national hymn?

At first, the words of "America the Beautiful" were put to different tunes, as these examples show. Katharine Lee Bates heard her poem sung to many compositions, but she would never say which one she liked best.

This was not the first time Bates's poem appeared in print. It was originally published in 1895—two years after her trip west—in *The Congregationalist*, a religious journal. Soon choirs throughout the country started putting the poem to music of all kinds. By the time the *Transcript* asked to reprint it, Bates had decided to rewrite some of the words "to make [the poem] a bit more musical."

"I just like that song immensely... 'America the Beautiful' is what I dream about America. It's the great experiment. It's the greatest country you could ever live in, because it's every nationality. It's not just one philosophy; it's every philosophy."

—Singer Tony Bennett

America, The Beautiful

KATHARINE LEE BATES   SAMUEL A. WARD

1. O beau - ti - ful for spa - cious skies, For am - ber waves of grain, — For
2. O beau - ti - ful for pil - grim feet Whose stern im - pas - sion'd stress, — A
3. O beau - ti - ful for he - roes prov'd In lib - er - at - ing strife, — Who
4. O beau - ti - ful for pa - triot dream That sees be - yond the years, — Thine

pur - ple moun - tain maj - es - ties A - bove the fruit - ed plain. — A -
thor - ough - fare for free - dom beat A - cross the wil - der - ness. — A -
more than self their coun - try loved, And mer - cy more than life. — A -
al - a - bas - ter cit - ies gleam Un - dimmed by hu - man tears. — A -

mer - i - ca! A - mer - i - ca! God shed His grace on thee, — And
mer - i - ca! A - mer - i - ca! God mend thine ev' - ry flaw, — Con -
mer - i - ca! A - mer - i - ca! May God thy gold re - fine — Till
mer - i - ca! A - mer - i - ca! God shed His grace on thee, — And

crown thy good with broth - er - hood From sea to shin - ing sea.
firm thy soul in self - con - trol, Thy lib - er - ty in law.
all suc - cess be no - ble - ness, And ev' - ry gain di - vine.
crown thy good with broth - er - hood From sea to shin - ing sea

One person who enjoyed the new version was Clarence A. Barbour. He was a minister in Rochester, New York. Barbour thought Bates's poem sounded like the **lyrics** to a hymn. Hymns are usually religious songs that praise God. This hymn, however, would be a song that praised a nation.

Barbour searched a hymnal for a song with a **rhythm** similar to that of the poem. Sam Ward's "Materna" was a perfect fit. Barbour introduced the music and lyrics to his church choir. Soon choirs in other communities began to sing the song. It grew even more popular when Barbour included it in a book of hymns he edited in 1910. The next year, Bates published her final version of the poem in her book *America the Beautiful and Other Poems.*

This sheet music shows Katharine Lee Bates's poem set to the music composed by Samuel Ward.

In 1917, the United States entered World War I (1914–1918). U.S. soldiers sent to fight in Europe carried small government-issued books of military and patriotic songs. One of the soldiers' favorites was "America the Beautiful." Civilians, too, sang it to show their love for the United States.

Unlike Sam Ward, Katharine Lee Bates lived to see her work become a beloved part of American culture. Four years after retiring from Wellesley, she died at her home in 1929. Bates was no doubt at peace with her life and her **legacy.** As she once wrote, "If I could write a poem people would remember after I'm dead, I would consider my life had been worth living."

Katharine Lee Bates spent her later years surrounded by family, friends, and many pets, including her dog, Hamlet.

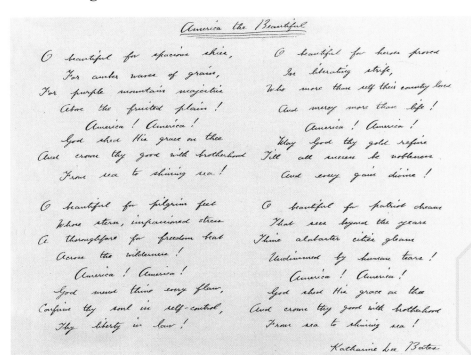

Bates handwrote this copy of "America the Beautiful." Among her friends and family, the poem became known as "A the B."

17

Revising the Song

Over the years, Katharine Lee Bates reworked the words to "America the Beautiful" several times. In 1911, she published her final version of the poem. It included small changes to every verse in the original poem. Some changes made the song easier to sing. For instance, in the first verse, "halcyon skies" became "spacious skies," and "enameled plains" became "fruited plains."

Other changes altered the poem's meaning. One such example appeared in the third verse. Bates's original poem celebrated the "glory-tale/of liberating strife"—which focused on American wars. In the final version, she instead hailed the "heroes proved,/in liberating strife." The change shifted Bates's praise to the brave soldiers who defended American freedoms on the battlefield.

"America the Beautiful," as first published in *The Congregationalist* in 1895:

O beautiful for halcyon skies,
For amber waves of grain,
For purple mountain majesties
Above the enameled plain!
America! America!
God shed his grace on thee
Till souls wax fair as earth and air
And music-hearted sea!

O beautiful for pilgrim feet,
Whose stern, impassioned stress
A thoroughfare for freedom beat
Across the wilderness!
America! America!
God shed his grace on thee
Till paths be wrought through
   wilds of thought
By pilgrim foot and knee!

O beautiful for glory-tale
Of liberating strife,
When once and twice, for man's avail,
Men lavished precious life!
America! America!
God shed his grace on thee
Till selfish gain no longer stain
The banner of the free!

O beautiful for patriot dream
That sees beyond the years
Thine alabaster cities gleam
Undimmed by human tears!
America! America!
God shed his grace on thee,
Till nobler men keep once again
Thy whiter jubilee!

"America the Beautiful," as Katharine Lee Bates revised it for the last time in 1911. We sing these words today:

O beautiful for spacious skies,
For amber waves of grain,
For purple mountain majesties
Above the fruited plain!
America! America!
God shed His grace on thee
And Crown thy good with brotherhood
From sea to shining sea!

O beautiful for pilgrim feet,
Whose stern, impassioned stress
A thoroughfare for freedom beat
Across the wilderness!
America! America!
God mend thine every flaw,
Confirm thy soul in self-control,
Thy liberty in law!

O beautiful for heroes proved
In liberating strife,
Who more than self their
   country loved,
And mercy more than life!
America! America!
May God thy gold refine
Till all success be nobleness
And every gain divine!

O beautiful for patriot dream
That sees beyond the years
Thine alabaster cities gleam
Undimmed by human tears!
America! America!
God shed His grace on thee
And crown thy good with brotherhood
From sea to shining sea!

What Do the Words Mean?

alabaster: smooth and white

amber: yellow or yellow-brown

brotherhood: goodwill among people

crown: to complete or make perfect

fruited: covered with fruit

liberty: freedom

majesties: things that are noble or grand

patriot: someone who loves his or her country

pilgrim: a traveler

refine: to improve or purify

spacious: vast; covering a large area

stress: physical pressure

strife: a struggle, conflict, or war

thoroughfare: a main road or passage

undimmed: not lessened or weakened

The Song's Meaning

When Katharine Lee Bates wrote "America the Beautiful," the United States was at a crossroads. In many ways, the nation had much to offer. In the 1800s, the size of the country had more than tripled. By the century's end, it stretched from the Atlantic Ocean to the Pacific Ocean—or "from sea to shining sea," as Bates wrote. As the country's size grew, so did its power. With its vast natural resources and thriving industries, the United States had become one of the wealthiest nations on the planet.

At the time Katharine Lee Bates wrote "America the Beautiful," U.S. industries were booming. Here, loggers harvest the valuable timber of the northwestern United States.

Many Americans lost their jobs and faced tough times in the mid-1890s. This crowd of unemployed workers marched from Ohio to Washington, D.C., to demand help from the government.

But the United States also had much to fear. When Bates wrote her poem, the country was in an economic depression. Many businesses had to close, and more than 2.5 million people lost their jobs. The poorest Americans were suffering greatly. At the same time, those who controlled America's large industries were growing ever richer. A troubling gap was growing between the few wealthy and the many poor.

"The song always made me feel good, always gave me goose bumps. It is a song about hopes and dreams…not only about our glorious past but about our infinite possibilities for the future."

—Lynn Sherr, author of
America the Beautiful: The Stirring True Story Behind Our Nation's Favorite Song

"America the Beautiful" praises the country's landscapes "from sea to shining sea."

Other people were concerned that the country's rapid growth had come to an end. Among them was historian Frederick Turner. He gave a speech to a crowd at the World's Columbian Exposition. Turner said that what had made America great was the energy and drive its people put into growing the nation. But by 1893, there was little land left for the United States to gain. Turner feared that without a **frontier** to conquer, America would lose its spirit and strength.

Like many Americans, Bates was thinking about how the country's future would take shape. Would it grow stronger, as people used new ideas and technologies to improve American life? Or would it become weaker, with the average American falling into poverty and hopelessness?

With such questions in mind, Bates wrote and rewrote the four verses of "America the Beautiful." The poem celebrates the natural beauty of America and the country's strength. But it also warns that greed and irresponsible behavior could pose a threat to America's greatness. In the end, though, Bates's poem is hopeful. She concludes that, with God's help, the country's future is bright.

In the poem's first four lines, Bates lists the marvelous sites she saw while traveling west. She writes of the "amber waves of grain" she spied from the train. She also praises the "spacious skies" and "purple mountain majesties/Above the fruited plain," remembering the view from Pikes Peak. The first verse ends as all four verses in the poem do—with a prayer. She asks God to "shed His grace" on the country and spread a sense of "brotherhood" among Americans.

The second verse celebrates the early American settlers. She calls them "pilgrim[s]" who blazed "a thoroughfare for freedom…across the wilderness." With these words, she praises the spirit of independence that allowed these pioneers to settle unfamiliar lands. In this verse's prayer, Bates hopes Americans can remain great by exercising "self-control" and making fair laws.

Bates honors America's war heroes in the poem's third verse. Because of their sacrifice, she explains, the United States has remained free. At the end of the verse, she prays that God will protect the country from greed. She hopes that financial success will bring out "nobleness," rather than selfishness, in the American people.

The final verse of "America the Beautiful" looks to the future. Bates speaks of "patriot dreams" for a better tomorrow. She imagines a future of "alabaster cities." With that phrase, Bates was possibly remembering the great White City she saw at the World's Columbian Exposition in Chicago. In Bates's vision, these cities will shine "undimmed by human tears." With this line, Bates admits that Americans will still feel pain and hopelessness in the future. But she also predicts that the United States will be able to survive such dark times.

Bates ends her poem with the same stirring prayer from its first verse: "America! America!/God shed His grace on thee/And crown thy good with brotherhood/From sea to shining sea."

The second verse of the song honors America's early pioneers, who braved harsh conditions to settle the country.

The Song Today

For nearly 20 years, Americans debated which patriotic song should become the national anthem. "The Star-Spangled Banner" was given this honor in 1931.

By the early 1900s, just about every American knew a few patriotic songs. Bands often played the lively ditty "Yankee Doodle Dandy" at picnics and parties. For more solemn occasions, they usually turned to "Hail Columbia" or "The Star-Spangled Banner." But for nearly any event, "America the Beautiful" seemed an appropriate **anthem.** With its simple melody and upbeat tone, it became the favorite patriotic tune of many Americans. Among them was Katharine Lee Bates's friend, novelist Albert Payson Terhune. He declared, "It IS America....I love every line of it...because it is poetry and noble."

In 1912, a bill came before the U.S. Congress. It called for "The Star-Spangled Banner" to become the national anthem. A national anthem is the official patriotic song of a country. It is played or sung at many public events—from government receptions to sporting events.

The bill did not pass, but it started a debate that lasted almost 20 years. Many people and organizations wanted "The Star-Spangled Banner" to be the national anthem. But just as many thought "America the Beautiful" was a better choice.

Those who favored "America the Beautiful" said it was much easier to sing. They also preferred its message. Bates's lyrics spoke of the country's great past and prayed for an even more glorious future. The story told in "The Star-Spangled Banner" was less meaningful for some Americans. Its lyrics told of the experiences of poet Francis Scott Key as he witnessed a battle during the War of 1812. Troublesome for many, too, was that the tune came from an English song often sung in taverns.

Despite such feelings, "The Star-Spangled Banner" officially became the national anthem in 1931. During her lifetime, Bates was happy to stay out of the debate. She wrote, "As to making ["America the Beautiful"] the national anthem, I am personally more than content with the heart-warming reception the song…has already had."

Indeed, the American public's affection for "America the Beautiful" has made it something of an unofficial national hymn. In good times, it allows us to celebrate the beauty and strength of our country. In bad times, it gives us confidence that the future will be brighter. Bates herself recognized the song's appeal for the American people. She wrote, "Americans are at heart **idealists,** with a fundamental faith in human brotherhood."

1 Coney Island: Visited by Samuel Ward on the day he composed the music to "America the Beautiful," this resort area is in Brooklyn, New York. It is famed for its seaside boardwalk, amusement park, and sideshows. Coney Island was especially popular with city-dwellers during the late 1800s and early 1900s, sometimes drawing up to a million people on a hot summer's day.

2 Niagara Falls: Niagara Falls straddles the border of western New York and Ontario, Canada. Upon seeing its two great waterfalls—the American Falls and the Horseshoe Falls—Katharine Lee Bates was awed by the beauty of America. Today, about 12 million tourists visit the falls each year. Helicopters, hot-air balloons, and boats provide visitors an up-close look at the falls.

3 World's Columbian Exposition: Held in Chicago in 1893, this "World's Fair" celebrated the 400 years that had passed since Christopher Columbus sailed to North America. It was also meant to show the world what a great nation the United States had become. The fair featured the fantastic "alabaster" buildings of the White City, as well as exhibits from every state and from 47 countries.

4 Kansas wheat fields: Kansas is still covered with "amber waves of grain," the same view Katharine Lee Bates saw from her train window more than 100 years ago. Nicknamed the Wheat State, Kansas today produces more wheat than any other state.

5 Pikes Peak: Pikes Peak in Colorado was named for Zebulon Pike, an American army officer who explored the Rocky Mountains in 1806. Standing 14,110 feet (4,301 meters) tall, the mountain is still famous for the "fruited plains" and "purple mountain majesties" seen from the peak. Today, visitors can reach the peak on foot, by car, or by railway.

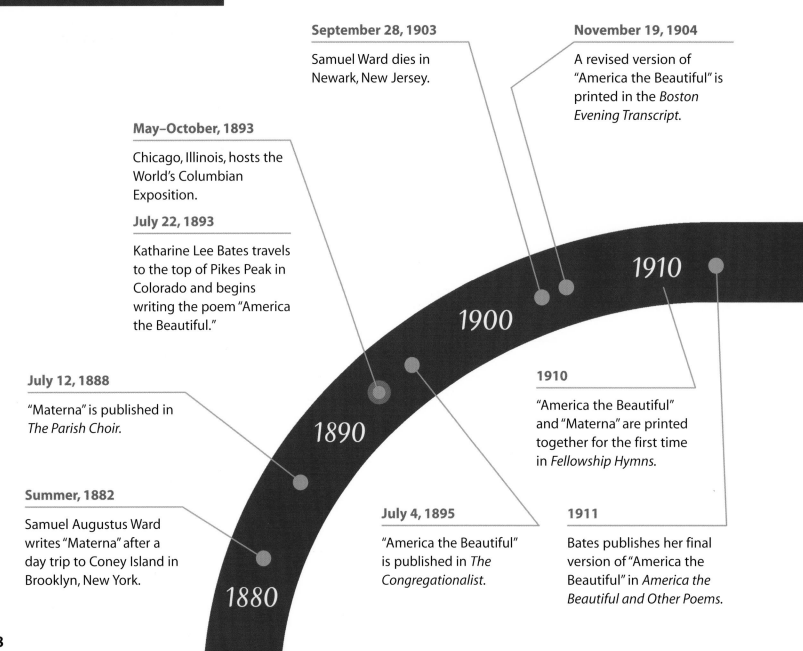

September 28, 1903

Samuel Ward dies in Newark, New Jersey.

November 19, 1904

A revised version of "America the Beautiful" is printed in the *Boston Evening Transcript*.

May–October, 1893

Chicago, Illinois, hosts the World's Columbian Exposition.

July 22, 1893

Katharine Lee Bates travels to the top of Pikes Peak in Colorado and begins writing the poem "America the Beautiful."

July 12, 1888

"Materna" is published in *The Parish Choir*.

Summer, 1882

Samuel Augustus Ward writes "Materna" after a day trip to Coney Island in Brooklyn, New York.

July 4, 1895

"America the Beautiful" is published in *The Congregationalist*.

1910

"America the Beautiful" and "Materna" are printed together for the first time in *Fellowship Hymns*.

1911

Bates publishes her final version of "America the Beautiful" in *America the Beautiful and Other Poems*.

1880

1890

1900

1910

Timeline

1917-1918
"America the Beautiful" gains popularity as the United States fights World War I.

March 28, 1929
Katharine Lee Bates dies in Wellesley, Massachusetts.

March 4, 1931
"The Star-Spangled Banner" becomes the official national anthem of the United States.

1976
People in Falmouth, Massachusetts, suggest that "America the Beautiful" be named the official bicentennial hymn.

1920   1930   1940   1950   1960   1970   1980

America in 1893

In 1893, a journey west inspired Katharine Lee Bates to write "America the Beautiful." What else was happening in the United States in 1893?

★ The United States is made up of 44 states.

★ The president is Grover Cleveland.

★ Stock prices drop, plunging America into a four-year economic depression.

★ U.S. troops overthrow Liliuokalani, the queen of Hawaii.

★ Dr. Daniel Hale Williams, a Chicago surgeon, performs the world's first open-heart surgery.

★ Cracker Jacks, soda pop, and the zipper are all introduced at the World's Columbian Exposition in Chicago.

★ Unemployed workers march on Washington, D.C., to demand that the government create new jobs.

★ The U.S. government opens millions of acres in Indian Territory (now Oklahoma) for settlement by non-Indians.

★ Henry Ford tests his first motorcar.

anthem (AN-thuhm) a patriotic song

exposition (ek-spuh-ZIH-shuhn) a public fair or show

frontier (fruhn-TEER) the far reaches of a country where few people live; until the late 1800s, much of the western United States was considered a frontier.

hymn (HIM) a song of praise, usually to God

hymnal (HIM-nuhl) a book of hymns

idealist (eye-DEE-uhl-ist) a person who has high standards of excellence that often cannot practically be met

legacy (LEG-uh-see) something that is handed down from one generation to another

lyrics (LEER-iks) words set to music

obituary (oh-BIT-chu-ayr-ee) a printed notice of a person's death

patriotic (pay-tree-AH-tik) having love for your country

professor (pruh-FESS-ur) a teacher at a college or university

rhythm (RITH-uhm) a regular beat or pattern of sounds

sojourn (SO-jern) a temporary stay

Students wave flags and sing "America the Beautiful" at a ceremony honoring the victims of the September 11, 2001, terrorist attacks.

To Learn More

READ THESE BOOKS

Bates, Katharine Lee. *America the Beautiful: The Complete Verses.* Berkeley, Calif.: Publishers Group West, 2001.

Fisher, Leonard Everett. *Niagara Falls: Nature's Wonder.* New York: Holiday House, 1996.

Frank, James. *A Portrait of Pikes Peak Country.* Canmore, Alberta: Altitude Publishing, 2000.

Sherr, Lynn. *America the Beautiful: The Stirring True Story Behind Our Nation's Favorite Song.* New York: Public Affairs, 2001.

Silverman, Jerry. *Of Thee I Sing: Lyrics and Music for America's Most Patriotic Songs.* New York: Citadel Press, 2002.

Sonneborn, Liz. *The Star-Spangled Banner: The Story Behind Our National Anthem.* Philadelphia: Chelsea Clubhouse, 2004.

Younger, Barbara. *Purple Mountain Majesties: The Story of Katharine Lee Bates and "America the Beautiful."* New York: Dutton, 1998.

LOOK UP THESE INTERNET SITES

History of Patriotic Songs
www.sbgmusic.com/html/teacher/reference/styles/patriotic.html
This site offers information about many of America's patriotic songs, including "America the Beautiful."

Katharine Lee Bates
www.vsg.cape.com/~1congfal/klbates.html
This site features a short biography of Bates and several of her poems.

Pikes Peak Cam
www.pikespeakcam.com
This web site broadcasts live views of Pikes Peak, taken by a camera positioned 15 miles (24 kilometers) from its summit.

Samuel Augustus Ward's "Materna"
www.cyberhymnal.org/htm/g/i/gisourrs.htm
This site includes a sound file of Ward's composition. Also featured are sound files of "Bethlehem" and "Winchester Old"—two of the many other songs paired with "America the Beautiful."

World's Columbian Exposition
xroads.virginia.edu/~MA96/WCE/tour.html
This site offers a tour of Chicago's great "World's Fair," the second stop on Katharine Lee Bates's trip.

INTERNET SEARCH KEY WORDS
America the Beautiful, Katharine Lee Bates, Samuel Augustus Ward

Index